THE
PUMPKIN
CARVING
BOOK

THE
PUMPKIN
CARVING
BOOK

Deborah Schneebeli-Morrell

♦♦♦

Photography by Debbie Patterson

♦♦♦

Text by Tessa Evelegh

LORENZ BOOKS
NEW YORK • LONDON • SYDNEY • BATH

This edition first published in 1996 by Lorenz Books,
an imprint of Anness Publishing Inc.
administration office: 27 West 20th Street
New York, NY10011

Lorenz Books are available for bulk purchase for sales promotion and
for premium use. For details, write or call the manager of special sales,
LORENZ BOOKS, 27 West 20th Street, New York, NY 10011; (212) 807-6739

Produced by Anness Publishing Limited
Hermes House
88-89 Blackfriars Road
London SE1 8HA

ISBN 1 85967 305 8

PUBLISHER: *Joanna Lorenz*
PROJECT EDITOR: *Judith Simons*
DESIGNER: *Annie Moss*
MAC ARTIST: *John Fowler*
PHOTOGRAPHER: *Debbie Patterson*
ILLUSTRATOR: *Annie Moss*

CONTENTS

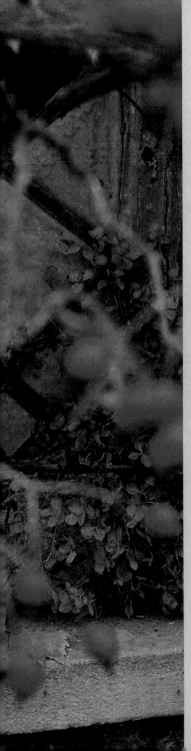

INTRODUCTION

Pumpkins and squashes, with their fiery colors and full, rounded shapes, are the very embodiment of autumn fruitfulness. They are the symbol of autumn, the principal players in harvest displays and at Halloween when they take the stage as Jack O'Lantern with his familiar triangular features. But pumpkins and their close cousins, the squashes and gourds, have so much more to offer in decorative terms. The sheer variety of shapes and colors seems endless. There are the elegant flattened shapes of white Patty Pans and pretty ridged ovals of Acorn squashes; there are pear, banana and full rounded shapes in golds, pinks, oranges and greens, and even the extraordinary two-tier forms of Turk's Turbans in green and orange stripes. They can be gathered together for fabulous seasonal displays, or particularly beautiful specimens can be placed on their own as exquisite organic decorations on the side table or hearth.

The rich assortment of shape and color in the pumpkin family provides a wonderful range of natural "canvases" for carving. Carved pumpkins no longer have to be confined to the huge orange varieties cut with ghoulish Halloween images. With a little imagination, you can give many other varieties decorative and figurative designs and make glorious seasonal displays for any celebration in the autumn or, indeed, for as long as the pumpkin is fresh and the flesh firm enough to cut.

Small night-light candles are often placed inside the hollowed-out shells of carved pumpkins, providing a warm glow while highlighting the design. The more complicated delicate patterns are usually cut just into the skin of the pumpkin, to become delightful decorations accentuated by the light inside. Simpler shapes can be cut right through the shell so that the brighter beams of light transform the pumpkin into an organic lamp. As well as traditional votive candles, you can use electric fairy lights or small lamps, although if a cord is involved you will need to cut a large hole in the underside of the pumpkin and lay the pumpkin over the light, rather than leaving the cord to trail untidily out of the top of the pumpkin. If using candles, make sure that the opening is in the top of the pumpkin and don't cover it with a lid, or else the pumpkin will burn.

Carving the pumpkin family is not a new craft. Decorated gourds have been found in Peruvian archaeological sites dating back to 2000 BC, and gourds have been carved with intricate designs for centuries in

ABOVE: *Pumpkins and pumpkin carving are traditionally associated with Halloween, when door steps and windows are aglow with Jack O'Lanterns.*

parts of the world as diverse as Africa, South America, Hawaii and New Zealand.

Pumpkins and squashes are thought to have evolved from the harder-skinned and less fleshy gourd, and their full-bodied shapes make them just as good for carving, using the same tools that have been used

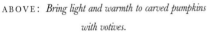

ABOVE: *Bring light and warmth to carved pumpkins*
with votives.

RIGHT: *Pumpkins and squashes come in a vast array of*
sizes and shapes.

for centuries – simple chisels and sharp knives. However, there is a difference in how pumpkins and squashes can be used. Unlike gourds, which quickly dry out to make lasting decorations or vessels, pumpkins are fleshy and retain moisture, so once they are cut they will only last for about a week before they begin to molder. The heat of the candles inside them hastens this process, so do not carve them too early before a celebration. The short lifespan of a carved pumpkin makes it all the more special; think of it like an elaborate flower arrangement, which you would never expect to last for more than a week. If you want to retain your design for posterity, you can always capture it in a photograph while it is still at its best.

The fact that pumpkins and squashes soon spoil once they are carved does not mean your skills have to be saved up for just a couple of weeks of the year. Kept in a cool place, some uncarved pumpkins will last the year round until the next harvest. Buy in a good supply while they are in season and you will have the raw material for unusual beautiful organic decorations for many months to come.

GUIDE TO PUMPKINS AND SQUASHES

The sheer variety of their shapes and colors makes pumpkins and squashes a delight to carve. However, the designs will be governed to a certain extent by the fruits themselves. Those with very hard flesh are difficult to hollow out and are best simply engraved on the surface; others with scoopable insides but hard skins can be pierced and drilled; while softer skins can be carved in a more intricate manner. The following are just a sample of the many varieties available and have all been used in the carving projects in this book.

The delicate mottled surface pattern of the Fig Leaf gourd disguises a hard skin. For this variety, it is best to scoop out the flesh, then cut simple shapes right through the skin.

Acorn squashes have reasonably soft skin and flesh, making them versatile subjects for carving. Their neat, regular ridges provide the perfect basis for a geometric design and the color of their skins ranges from green, through yellow to golden.

The firm innards of the highly colored Turk's Turban, make it hard to scoop out, so it is best to keep your design to simple lino-cut lines and drilled holes.

The Melonette St. Julien has a smooth, soft skin, and the flesh is easy to scoop out. The smaller Crown of Thorns has rock hard flesh and it is best to use it uncarved as an accessory to a main display.

The delightful small Baby Red Hubburd squash has a hard flesh, but its onion shape and bright red color make it a perfect choice for a small Jack O'Lantern.

The Banana squash is soft and easy to carve and its unusual elongated shape gives variety to any display. Use it lying down, or shave off the bottom for a tall upright form.

The stunningly beautiful White Boer pumpkin has solid flesh that is difficult to hollow out. Use it as a "canvas" for engraving a simple design or, if you have the skills, an exquisite picture.

The wonderful cushion shape and glorious red glow of the Rouge Vif d'Etampes pumpkin, combined with its easy to carve flesh and skin, make it a perfect candidate for decoration.

Patty Pan squashes have a flat dish-like shape which means they are very difficult to hollow out, but their pretty deckle edges and delicate shades are perfect for surface decoration.

The Sweet Dumpling gourd has a wonderful variegated green skin, and a hard but sweet orange flesh.

The bright orange shades of Halloween pumpkins are familiar to all and readily available during the autumn months.

CARVING TECHNIQUES

The appeal of pumpkin carving is that anyone can do it. All you need is a pumpkin, a few simple tools that you may well find around the house and garden, and away you go. Once you gain confidence and enthusiasm, however, you will probably want to tackle more intricate patterns and buy a few tools specially for the job.

There is a great variety in the texture of the flesh and skins of the different varieties of pumpkins and squashes. The Guide to Pumpkins and Squashes indicates the types of designs suitable for the different kinds of pumpkins, and many of them are clearly demonstrated in the step-by-step projects. We do hope that the exquisitely carved pumpkins shown throughout the book will inspire you to try the art of pumpkin carving yourself.

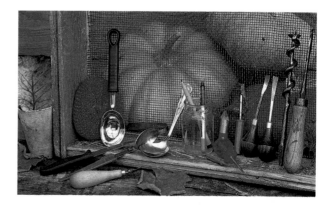

ABOVE: *The assortment of tools you will need to produce any of the pumpkin carvings shown in this book is not huge and most items will be found in the kitchen or tool box.*

Tools

The tools you will need fall into four main categories:

Toppers and tailers: You need a large kitchen knife for cutting off the tops and sometimes the bottoms of the pumpkins. A special pumpkin saw or small hacksaw is also useful for this. A saw is also sometimes used for cutting right through the side of the pumpkin as part of the design. A small, sharp kitchen knife is useful for cutting pretty zigzag tops for the pumpkins.

Scoopers: An ice-cream scoop is useful, plus a battery of kitchen spoons. For pumpkins with very hard flesh, you may need to use a woodcarving tool to chisel out the innards. A nylon pot scourer helps to smooth the inside once it has been hollowed out.

Markers: A water-soluble crayon is useful for marking out large designs, and a fine black pen for the more intricate patterns or for transferring templates. Dressmaker's pins are used to fix paper patterns and templates to the pumpkins, and a pricking tool or large needle to transfer designs.

Cutters and drillers: Drills, bradawls, gimlets and apple corers are useful for making holes of various sizes. Craft knives or scalpels can be used for finer cut-out designs or larger engraved designs, and woodcarving tools and lino-cutting tools for carving the surface of the pumpkin skin.

Getting started

First cut off the top or bottom of the pumpkin using a large kitchen knife or pumpkin saw. You may also want to level the bottom, if it is to stay intact, so that the pumpkin stands firm.

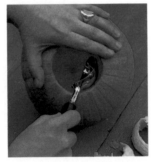

ABOVE: *First cut a circular hole in the top or bottom of the pumpkin with a kitchen knife or pumpkin saw.*

ABOVE: *Hollow out the interior of the pumpkin with a kitchen spoon or ice-cream scoop.*

Hollowing out

With soft-fleshed pumpkins, this is easy to do using kitchen spoons. Firmer flesh can be removed with an ice-cream scoop; hard fruits may even have to be hollowed out with the help of a knife or woodcarving tool. It is important that the remaining walls are about 1 in thick and have a smooth surface as this makes for a much neater finish and allows the light to shine through evenly. Test the thickness of the walls with a pin, poking it through in several places to a depth of 1 in. Finish smoothing the inside of the pumpkin with a nylon pot scourer.

Transferring the pattern

1 Choose simple patterns at first and be guided by the shape and size of the pumpkin or squash, perhaps drilling holes in grooves or along ridges.

On smoother pumpkins, you could try a straightforward geometric design.

2 As you progress to more complicated patterns, one of the problems you will meet is wrapping a flat design around a round pumpkin. One solution is to use smaller motifs all over the pumpkin; or you could have focal motifs at the back and front of the pumpkin set in geometric panels.

3 Motifs can be fixed to the pumpkin with dressmaker's pins and transferred by outlining them with a fine black pen or pricking out the design

with a pricking tool or large needle.

Carving

1 If any holes need to be drilled – whether they are for eyes or other facial features, or simply as part of the design – they are usually done first. If you are using a large drill bit, first wind it into the pumpkin, then withdraw it by carefully winding back to prevent damaging the edges of the holes.

2 Where you are cutting shapes right through the shell of the pumpkin, use a pumpkin saw or a small hacksaw for hard-skinned pumpkins and a sharp craft knife for those with softer skins.

ABOVE: *Revive a carved pumpkin that may be looking a little dried out before putting it on display by soaking it in water for two to eight hours.*

3 Designs engraved on to the surface of the pumpkin can be cut in much the same way as in lino-cutting, using a selection of lino-cutting or woodcarving tools.

Storing

As soon as the pumpkin has been carved, rub the cut areas with vegetable oil or petroleum jelly to delay ageing. Store the pumpkins in the refrigerator to keep them fresh until they are ready to be displayed. It is best not to carve them more than a day before they are needed, but if they do dry out a little, you can revive them by soaking them in water for two to eight hours, then thoroughly drying them once you take them out.

Growing your own

Pumpkins, squashes and gourds are astonishing in their growth. Starting from seed in mid-spring under glass, they grow into vigorous vines, reaching 9 m (30 ft) in length, even in cooler climes. And from behind the fertilized female flowers, the swelling bulb of the fruit almost visibly balloons out by the day.

This rapid growth lends the plant an exotic quality, and can put people off even trying to grow pumpkins for fear of failure. This is a shame because many varieties are not difficult to cultivate and their glorious leafy rambling quality makes them excellent for many situations – in the border or trained over a pergola or arbor, for example.

It is best to sow the seeds in small seed pots in an electric propagator set at about 75°F. The seeds should germinate in about six days, and any that have not sprouted within ten should be thrown away. Once they have germinated, take the pots out of the propagator and keep them in the greenhouse at about 65°F for about four weeks. Then, from the end of spring, harden them off in a cold frame and gradually open it up to allow more air in each day. When the threat of any late frost is past, you should be able to plant the pumpkins outside. If you want to train the plants up a pergola, arbor, or even trellis, start doing so as soon as the plants are large enough to tie into position. Once they are 8 ft long, pinch out the leading shoot to encourage the plant to thicken out. Pumpkins produce both male and female flowers. The female flowers will produce fruit once they are pollinated. It is best to

ABOVE: *If you have the space, don't be afraid to try cultivating pumpkins from seed. Many varieties are quite easy to grow.*

restrict the larger pumpkins to just two fruit and smaller squashes to about five, so pinch out any subsequent young fruits.

Any pumpkins that are not ripe by the time there is the threat of frost should be covered with a cloche or large piece of polythene. When they are ready to be cut, use a sharp knife to avoid wrenching or twisting and thus damaging the fruit.

IN THE LIMELIGHT

The soft buttermilk shades and handy size of Golden Acorn squash make them ideal for converting into simple organic lights. They are incredibly easy to make, and you don't need to be a master carver to pierce the simple holes through which the light shines through.

YOU WILL NEED

Water-soluble crayon

Golden Acorn squash

Kitchen knife

Ice-cream scoop

Teaspoon

Gimlet

◆ ◆ ◆

1 Using the crayon, mark out a large square on one side of the squash. Cut out and remove this part of the squash wall using the kitchen knife. When it is eventually laid on its side, this will be the bottom.

2 First using the ice-cream scoop and then the teaspoon, scrape out the seeds and flesh, making sure you clean out along the ridges. The shell should be about $\frac{1}{2}$ in thick.

3 Using the gimlet, make lines of holes along the furrows of the squash.

SMALL AND SWEET

Keep carving simple on the smaller pumpkins, lending variety with slits, zigzags and scrolls. Make several, then group them in an evocative autumnal window display.

YOU WILL NEED

Fine black pen
Small pumpkins/squash
Craft knife
Teaspoon

◆ ◆ ◆

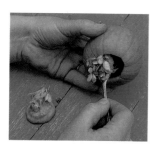

1 Using the pen, draw a circle on the base of each pumpkin. Cut out using the craft knife. Scoop out the flesh with the teaspoon.

2 Draw zigzags on one pumpkin and cut away with the craft knife. The slits should be ¼ in wide in the middle, tapering to points at both ends.

3 Draw and cut straight slits on another pumpkin. For the scroll design, first draw on the shape, then carefully cut away using the craft knife.

ZIGZAG

Furrows feature on many pumpkins and squashes, and by working with the ridge lines you can achieve simple but striking designs. This green Acorn squash was given an allover geometric look, which was enhanced with pierced holes to let the light gleam through.

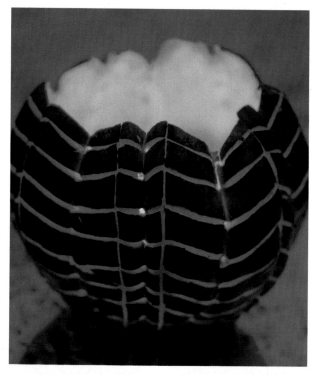

YOU WILL NEED

Water-soluble crayon

Green Acorn squash

Kitchen knife

Ice-cream scoop

Woodcarving tool

Lino-cutting tool

Bradawl

1 Using the crayon, draw around the top of the squash, following the ridges and furrows to give a zigzag outline. Cut out using the kitchen knife. Use the ice-cream scoop to remove the flesh. Finish off with the woodcarving tool, leaving a shell ½ in thick.

2 Using the lino-cutting tool, cut lines down the ridges and then make zigzag lines between them.

3 Using the bradawl, pierce holes in the furrows where the cut lines meet.

PALE BEAUTY

An elegant squash in palest green has an almost luminous quality about it and needs only a few carved holes to transform it into a captivating autumn light.

1 Using the crayon, draw a circle on the top of the squash about 3½ in in diameter. Cut out using the pumpkin saw and then scoop out the seeds with your hands. Using the woodcarving tool, chip and carve away at the solid orange flesh until the shell is no more than ¾ in thick. This may take some time.

2 Holding the drill bit in your hand, pierce through the shell using a pushing and twisting action. Once it is through, remove it by twisting it back in a counterclockwise direction so you do not damage the skin around the hole.

SNOWFLAKE

If pumpkins are still around when the snow arrives, it is lovely to echo the season by carving a snowflake motif. You will need a large pumpkin that will offer enough surface space to incorporate the detail of this design.

YOU WILL NEED

Water-soluble crayon

Rouge Vif d'Etampes pumpkin

Kitchen knife

Ice-cream scoop

Lino-cutting tool

Bradawl

◆ ◆ ◆

2 Using the ice-cream scoop, remove the seeds and flesh. Then draw four evenly spaced dots around the circumference of the pumpkin.

1 Using the crayon, draw a circle on the top of the pumpkin. Cut out the lid using the kitchen knife.

3 Use these marks for the center of each snowflake. Using the crayon, draw in each snowflake, starting with a star shape. Draw a smaller star between them. Using the lino-cutting tool, cut out the large stars.

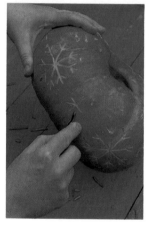

4 Using the same tool, add branches to the large stars to create snowflakes, then cut out the small stars.

5 Using the bradawl, pierce a hole in the center of each snowflake and star, and also at the points where the branches meet. Pierce a circle of holes around each snowflake and around the top opening.

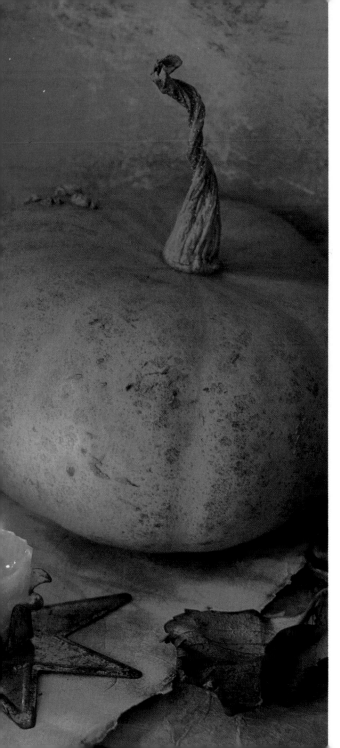

PERFECT GEOMETRY

Choose a geometric design made up of alternating bands of simple motifs for an intricate effect.

1 Using the crayon, draw a circle on the top of the squash. Cut it out with the small pumpkin saw.

YOU WILL NEED ·

Water-soluble crayon

Pink-skinned squash
or pumpkin

Pumpkin saw

Ice-cream scoop

Nylon pot scourer

Lino-cutting tool

Craft knife

Flat-edged
woodcarving tool

Woodcarving scoop ·

◆ ◆ ◆

2 Using the ice-cream scoop, hollow out the inside, leaving a shell about ¾ in thick. Smooth the inside using the pot scourer and rinse out.

▶

27

PERFECT GEOMETRY

3 Draw a series of concentric patterns round the squash and a simple sunflower shape on the base.

4 Using the lino-cutting tool, cut the straight lines, petal shapes and stars.

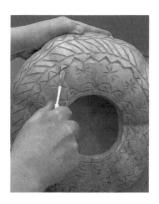

5 To cut out the triangles, start by cutting each side with the craft knife. Lift out the triangles with the flat-edged woodcarving tool.

6 On the base, use the woodcarving scoop to cut out the "seeds" on the sunflower shape.

TURK'S TURBAN AND SWEET DUMPLING LANTERN

The natural two-tier form of the Turk's Turban makes a perfect base for this lantern. Generously pierced with holes, it creates a delightful shining lamp.

YOU WILL NEED

Water-soluble crayon

Turk's Turban and Sweet Dumpling gourd

Pumpkin saw

Woodcarving tool

Lino-cutting tool

Gimlet

Ice-cream scoop

Kitchen spoon

Kitchen knife

◆ ◆ ◆

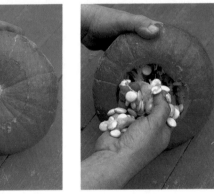

1 Use the crayon to draw a circle on the base of the Turk's Turban squash, about 4–4¾ in across, to accommodate the Sweet Dumpling gourd. Cut out using the pumpkin saw.

2 Scoop out the seeds with your hand. Next, the flesh has to be scooped out. Because Turk's Turban flesh is very hard, you will probably need to use the woodcarving tool to chip away at it. It is important to remove the flesh evenly from the larger orange part of the squash.

3 Draw a curly design around the larger part of the squash. Cut along the drawn lines with the lino-cutting tool.

▶

▶

29

TURK'S TURBAN AND
SWEET DUMPLING LANTERN

4 Using the gimlet, pierce evenly spaced holes all around the stripy-colored part of the Turk's Turban.

6 Using the gimlet, make lines of holes along the furrows of the Sweet Dumpling. Use the kitchen knife to cut slits along the tops of the ridges to let shafts of light through.

5 Draw a circle on the top and base of the Sweet Dumpling gourd; the base opening should be marginally smaller than the opening in the top of the Turk's Turban. Cut out using the pumpkin saw. Use the ice-cream scoop and kitchen spoon to hollow out the gourd to a thickness of about ½ in.

30

EASTER PARADE

Folk-art roosters strutting around this starlit pumpkin make for a charming design. It is delightful at any time of the year, but makes a particularly original Easter display if you can save a pumpkin for long enough.

YOU WILL NEED

Water-soluble crayon

Peach-skinned pumpkin

Pumpkin saw

Ice-cream scoop

Kitchen spoon

Lino-cutting tool

Craft knife

Flat-edged
woodcarving tool

Dressmaker's pins

Fine black pen

Gimlet

♦ ♦ ♦

1 Using the crayon, draw a circle on the top of the pumpkin. Cut out using the pumpkin saw. Using the ice-cream scoop and kitchen spoon, remove the seeds and flesh. Draw two parallel lines around the body of the pumpkin about 4 in apart. Cut along these lines using the lino-cutting tool.

2 Using the craft knife, cut the sides of the triangles freehand, then lift them out using the flat-edged woodcarving tool.

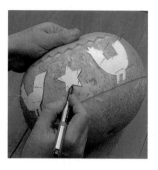

3 Trace the templates from the back of the book and enlarge if necessary. Pin in position and draw around them using the pen.

4 Remove the templates then cut out the shapes, slicing through the pumpkin with the craft knife.

5 Using the gimlet, make holes between the roosters and stars as shown.

LETTERS
AND NUMBERS

Letters and numbers in different typefaces make an appealing design when arranged over the surface of a pumpkin. Use the templates at the back of the book, or make up your own by enlarging letters and numbers from magazines and newspapers on a photocopier.

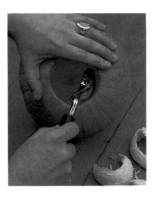

1 Use the crayon to draw a circle on the top of the pumpkin, then cut out using the pumpkin saw. Scoop out the flesh evenly with the ice-cream scoop and kitchen spoon, leaving a shell about ³/₄ in thick.

2 Trace the letter and number templates from the back of the book and enlarge if necessary. Fix the templates in position on the pumpkin with dressmaker's pins. Using the pen, draw around the templates.

3 Using the craft knife, carefully cut out the letters and numbers.

FELINE FRIENDS

Pale-skinned pumpkins make marvelous "canvases" for all sorts of characters. This design provides a witty twist to the traditional Halloween witch's cat.

1 Trace the template from the back of the book and enlarge if necessary. Fix the template over the base of the pumpkin with dressmaker's pins. Using the pumpkin pricking tool or a large needle, make small pin pricks along all the lines.

YOU WILL NEED

White Boer pumpkin

Dressmaker's pins

Pumpkin pricking tool, or large needle

Lino-cutting tool

2 Using the lino-cutting tool, carve the design on to the pumpkin, following the lines of pin pricks. Cut short lines for the cat's fur.

FOLK-ART FLOWER URNS

Large motifs like this charming potted plant are easy to accommodate on unforgiving curves if you first divide the pumpkin or squash into panels. These panels can then be decorated with simple geometric patterns such as the cross-hatched diagonals used here.

YOU WILL NEED

Water-soluble crayon

Green-skinned squash

Pumpkin saw

Ice-cream scoop

Kitchen spoon

Lino-cutting tool

Dressmaker's pins

Pumpkin pricking tool, or large needle

1 Use the crayon to draw a small circle on the top of the squash. Cut out using the pumpkin saw. Use the ice-cream scoop and kitchen spoon to scoop out the flesh.

2 Mark the squash into quarters with the crayon. Draw parallel lines close to the original lines, then draw another set of parallel lines near these to create the boundaries of the panels. Mark a cross-hatched pattern between these lines. Use the lino-cutting tool to cut the panel lines and the cross-hatched pattern.

3 Trace the template from the back of the book and enlarge if necessary. Use dressmaker's pins to fix the template to the squash, then use the pumpkin pricking tool or a large needle to make small pin pricks along all the lines.

4 Use the lino-cutting tool to cut the flower urn design, following the lines of pin pricks. Repeat the pricking and cutting process for each section of the squash.

PRETTY AS A PATTY PAN

The deckle edge and pale shades of Patty Pans make them a delight to decorate, but their flat shape makes them difficult to hollow out. If you would like to give them a glow, cut them away at the back so that candle light can shine through from behind.

YOU WILL NEED

Patty Pan squash

Water-soluble crayon

Lino-cutting tool

Kitchen knife

Ice-cream scoop

◆ ◆ ◆

2 If you want to shine a light through the squash, cut away the back using the sharp kitchen knife. Scrape out the solid inner flesh with the ice-cream scoop, leaving a shell ¾ in thick.

1 Following the squash's flower-like form, carefully draw a design on the front using the crayon. Then, use the lino-cutting tool to cut neatly along the lines of your design.

STARS AND CURLS

This loose arabesque design is perfectly suited to curling around the smooth curved surface of a large pumpkin. Stars between the tendrils create a pretty overall pattern of movement and line.

YOU WILL NEED

Water-soluble crayon

Halloween pumpkin

Pumpkin saw
or kitchen knife

Ice-cream scoop

Kitchen spoon

Lino-cutting tool

◆ ◆ ◆

1 Using the crayon, draw a circle on the top of the pumpkin. Cut out the lid with the pumpkin saw or kitchen knife. Use the ice-cream scoop and kitchen spoon to scoop out the seeds and flesh, leaving a shell about 3/4 in thick. Draw a freehand tendril pattern all over the pumpkin. Add stars between the tendrils.

2 Use the lino-cutting tool to cut along the drawn lines.

3 Using the same tool, cut out the stars.

FALLING
LEAVES

The orange candlelight inside this pumpkin gives a warm autumnal glow to the falling leaves, which are thrown into bright relief against the the mottled green skin.

2 Scoop out the seeds and flesh using the ice-cream scoop and kitchen spoon.

4 Trace the templates from the back of the book and enlarge if necessary. Fix the templates to the gourd with dressmaker's pins. Draw around them with the pen.

5 Hold the gourd firmly and use the gimlet to make a hole inside the line of each leaf. Insert the pumpkin saw in the hole and carefully cut out the leaf shape. ▶

1 Using the crayon, draw a circle on the top of the gourd. Cut out the lid using the pumpkin saw.

3 The inside needs to be very smooth for this design, so rub it with the nylon pot scourer and rinse out.

45

FALLING LEAVES

6 Using the gimlet, make holes in the gourd between the leaves.

7 If you want to hang up the lantern, make a hole either side of the top and attach a wire loop.

FISH
CANDLEHOLDER

YOU WILL NEED

Banana squash

Masking tape

Pumpkin pricking tool,
or large needle

Lino-cutting tool

3 candles

Fine black pen

Craft knife

Woodcarving tool

◆ ◆ ◆

1 Trace the template from
the back of the book and
enlarge or reduce the design
to fit the squash. Use
masking tape to fix the
design on the squash.

2 Use the pumpkin pricking
tool or large needle to make
small pin pricks along all the
lines of the design. ▶

*This long slim pumpkin is the perfect shape to carve into
a fish. The lines are so simple, even the least artistically
inclined will come up with a brilliantly finished result.*

47

FISH
CANDLEHOLDER

3 Use the lino-cutting tool to carve the design, following the lines of pin pricks on the squash.

4 Use the lino-cutting tool to cut and lift a small dot on each fish scale. Repeat the design on the other side.

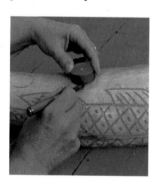 

5 Position a candle on top of the squash and to one end, and draw around it with the pen. Repeat twice to make a row down the fish's back.

6 Using the craft knife, cut around these lines and lift out the plug with the woodcarving tool. Make the holes deep enough to hold the candles securely.

TRIANGLES AND TEXTURE

Nothing could be simpler than carving triangles between concentric rings around a squash. Yet when they are cut through dark skin to reveal pale flesh, the result is this stunning textural allover design.

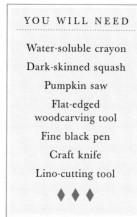

1 Using the crayon, draw a circle on the top of the squash. Cut out using the pumpkin saw. Chip out the very firm flesh from the inside using the wood-carving tool.

2 Turn the squash upside down and use the pen to draw concentric circles around the squash.

3 Draw lines between these rings to create triangles. Using the craft knife, cut neatly around each triangle, making sure you do not slice too deeply.

4 Cut out the top circle with the lino-cutting tool. Using the flat-edged woodcarving tool, cut away the triangles of skin and carefully lift them out.

RUSSIAN HOUSE

This traditional Russian-style folk-art house makes a delightful motif for any pumpkin. Carve one on each side of the pumpkin with potted trees between to create an allover design.

YOU WILL NEED

Water-soluble crayon

Halloween pumpkin

Kitchen knife

Ice-cream scoop

Dressmaker's pins

Pumpkin pricking tool, or large needle

Lino-cutting tool

◆ ◆ ◆

1 Using the crayon, draw a circle on the top of the pumpkin. Cut out using the kitchen knife. Scoop out the inside flesh and seeds with the ice-cream scoop.

2 Trace the templates from the back of the book and enlarge if necessary. Pin the house template to the pumpkin.

3 Use the pumpkin pricking tool or large needle to make small pin pricks along all the lines.

4 Use the lino-cutting tool to carve the design, following the lines of pin pricks on the pumpkin.

5 Repeat the whole process with the potted tree template, positioning it on either side of the house. Carve another house on the back of the pumpkin if there is room.

JACK O'LANTERN

Let everyone carve a different Halloween face to create a whole crowd of characters. Give them hats if you like, such as Jack's small pumpkin bobble hat.

YOU WILL NEED

Water-soluble crayon

Baby Red Hubbard and
a smaller squash

Kitchen knife

Ice-cream scoop

Fine black pen

Craft knife

Gimlet

Lino-cutting tool

◆ ◆ ◆

1 Using the crayon, draw a circle about 3½ in in diameter on the top of the Baby Red Hubbard squash. Cut out using the kitchen knife. Scoop out the seeds and flesh with the ice-cream scoop, leaving a shell ½ in thick. Draw the features on to one side of the squash with the pen.

2 Using the craft knife, cut the nose and eyebrows in one line. Cut away the whites of the eyes. Use the gimlet to make a hole in the center of each eye.

3 Use the lino-cutting tool to cut out the mustache. Cut the space between the teeth with the craft knife.

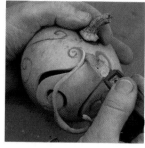

4 Cut out a circle in the base of the small pumpkin. and hollow out. Draw scrolls on the pumpkin.

5 Use the craft knife to cut the scrolls into curling slits.

FOLK HEART

Hearts make a pretty motif for almost anything: a full rounded pumpkin calls for a generous heart. This one has been decorated in the traditional Swiss style.

1 Using the crayon, draw a circle on the top of the pumpkin. Cut out with the kitchen knife. Scoop out the seeds and flesh using the ice-cream scoop and kitchen spoon, leaving a shell $1/2$ in thick. Draw a scalloped edge around the opening and cut it away using the craft knife.

2 Trace the template from the back of the book and enlarge if necessary. Fix the template to the front of the pumpkin with dressmaker's pins. Use the pumpkin pricking tool or a large needle to make small pin pricks along all the lines of the design.

3 Use the lino-cutting tool to carve out the design, following the pin prick lines.

4 Draw freehand branches either side of the heart to create a frame. Use the lino-cutting tool to carve the leaves as shown.

THE WISE WITCH

Carve an elegant witchy face to make a change from the traditional style, then crown your witch with a wreath of twigs for an exquisite Halloween or autumn decoration.

YOU WILL NEED

Water-soluble crayon

Halloween pumpkin

Kitchen knife

Ice-cream scoop

Pumpkin pricking tool
or large needle

Craft knife

Gimlet

Twig wreath

◆ ◆ ◆

1 Using the crayon, draw a circle on the top of the pumpkin. Cut out the lid using the kitchen knife and hollow out the inside with the ice-cream scroop.

2 Use the drawing of the face at the back of the book as a reference and copy directly on to the pumpkin. Wipe off any mistakes with a damp cloth. Dry the surface before redrawing. Alternatively, prick out the outlines of the design on to the pumpkin using a pumpkin pricking tool or large needle. Using the craft knife, cut each line into a narrow slit.

3 Cut away the whites of the eyes, leaving the irises and eye lid intact.

4 Use the gimlet to make holes in the centers of the eyes for pupils.

TEMPLATES

If the templates need to be enlarged or reduced in size to fit your chosen pumpkin, either use a grid system or a photocopier. For the grid system, trace the template and draw a grid of evenly spaced squares over your tracing. To scale up or down, draw a larger or smaller grid of the same number of squares on another piece of paper. Copy the outline on to the second grid by taking each square individually and drawing the relevant part of the outline in the larger or smaller square. For tracing templates, you will need tracing paper, a pencil, cardboard or paper and scissors.

EASTER PARADE PP 32-33

LETTERS AND NUMBERS PP 34-35

FOLK-ART FLOWER URNS PP 38-39

FELINE FRIENDS PP 36-37

FALLING LEAVES PP 44-46

RUSSIAN HOUSE PP 52-53

RUSSIAN HOUSE PP 52-53

FISH CANDLEHOLDER PP 47-49

FOLK HEART PP 56-57

THE WISE WITCH PP 58-59

INDEX

ACKNOWLEDGMENTS

The publishers and Tessa Evelegh would like to thank Ray Waterman, President of the World Pumpkin Confederation, and C R Upton for their invaluable help in identifying the pumpkins, squashes and gourds. Thanks are also due to C R Upton for providing pumpkins and space for photography.